"Hey, kids," Dad shouted to Luke and Linda, "bring your sand toys and hop in the car. We're going to Pismo Beach on the Central Coast. The trip really isn't that far."

"Unlike the big cities, it's quiet and pleasant,
with no heavy traffic any time.
Ocean-cooled in the summer and warmed in the winter,
the weather's unusually fine."

Welcome To
SAN LUIS OBISPO
COUNTY

From the window in their room where
Mom and Dad chose to stay,
the children saw pelicans and seagulls soaring, whales
spouting and smiling dolphins at play.

With shovels and pails--plus their toy boat with sails --
they ran to the beach with glee.
It was awesome fun to play in the sun where the smooth,
clean sand meets the sea.

When the tide was low at the waters edge,
small crabs scurried about.
"Look at them run fast. Wow, these tide pools are a blast,"
Luke and Linda would shout.

They went boogie boarding and kayaking,
then tried out surfboards, too.
The gentle waves were easy to ride…

Well, except for a few!

They walked way out on the long wooden pier.
With people catching fish and surfers riding waves,
there's no better place to see action than out here.

As they looked across the water
at the bluff along the shore,
they could feel the ocean mist
and hear the sea lions roar.

11

On a surrey-bike they peddled
down a classic beach-town street.
There were kites to buy, skateboards to try
and t-shirts and caps that are neat.

From great burgers, tacos, pizza--even bread-bowls of
clam chowder--to sushi, fresh fish and barbequed meats,
this place has it all when it comes to good meals...
plus fresh taffy and other snack treats.

They took the boardwalk to Pismo State Beach park.
Luke said, "Sometime let's camp here in a tent
when it's dark."
There are showers and picnic tables for each guest.
RVers and campers call it "paradise."
Being at the beach is the best.

Nearby is the famous butterfly grove
where thousands of Monarchs meet.
They cling to eucalyptus trees in the soft ocean breeze.
Yes, Cental Coast nature is neat!

In the center of town, along historic California Highway 1,
they came across something great:
classic old automobiles at the biggest
car show in the state.

There were '57 Chevys, old Buicks
and Corvettes, even some model-T Fords,
plus some woody station wagons
carrying old time surf-riding boards.

At Dinosaur Park, Luke and Linda climbed
on "pre-historic" eggs to play.
Meanwhile Mom and Dad found a painting they liked
at the outdoor artists' display.

While Luke and Dad joined a pickup team and played a game of beach volleyball, Linda and Mom hunted for super bargains at the giant outlet mall.

A breakfast bun baker, a glass jewelry maker,
a house with a windmill, too.
The family learned whatever you like,
it's here to see or to do.

19

They took the Bob Jones Bike Trail to Avila Beach
and stopped along the way
to look at a golf course near the ocean that
visitors love to play.

Next it was time for a fun ride with
a gentle horse for each.
Then... a visit to California's only park where ATVs climb
the dunes and cars can drive on the beach.

21

They rented a sportboat at Lopez Lake
in the nearby countryside
where there's a waterpark for family fun
with a super-thrilling slide.

Driving past beautiful vineyards planted
in evenly spaced lines,
they stopped to enjoy a close look at the
grapes hanging from the vines.

Everyone liked the famous Hearst Castle near the coast just a few miles away.

24

And...a farm wagon ride at Avila Beach
made it a very special day.

After a hike to the top of the bluff
overlooking scenic San Luis Bay,
they saw the very old lighthouse that helps
ocean ships find their way.

They found an ice cream parlor
and a swinging bridge in old town Arroyo Grande,
and berries the size of apples at a farmer's
strawberry stand.

And, not very far from Oceano's awesome dunes, it was family fun at a the Melodrama theater with its wacky plays and tunes.

Here on the friendly Central Coast the fun never ends day or night.

"There's entertainment with great things to do," Mom said. "It's a family vacation delight."

When it was time to go home, Luke and Linda said goodbye to other children they had met. "We had such a great time," said Louie from London, whose family came by train to Grover Beach after flying to California by jet.